The 60th Book of Prison Hope

Time for Purpose Plans

Rev. Mike Wanner

Copyright
Rev. Mike Wanner, July 21, 2018

Selected Images Used by License

Table of Contents

Copyright 2
Table of Contents 3
Introduction 4
1 - Why I Am Writing This Book 5
2 - The Power of Purpose 6
3 - Prisons Seem to Amplify a Down Spiral 7
4 - Concept Books Show Options 8
5 - What Options Have No Cost 9
6 - Why Space Matters 10
7 - Why Time Matters 11
8 - Why Self-Determination Matters 13
9 - Shift Blocks 14
10 - Thinking Change Can Create Hope 15
11 - Skill Set Inventory 16
12 - Single Unit Startup 17
13 - Every Prison Can Work at Changing 18
14 - Visitation & Motivation 20
15 - Prison Rehabilitation 21
16 - Prisoner Prayer 23
17 - Prayer Suggestion For Staff 24
18 - Envision Please an Up Spiral 25
19 - Wrap Up 26
20 - Thank You 27
21 - Don't Worry Ever 28
22 - Books Category Resources 29
23 - Angels Please Prayers 30
24 - Private Channeling 31
25 - Reverend Mike Wanner 32

Introduction

In late April/Early May 2013, I was contacted by a friend, student, and teacher and was told that she wanted to channel for me. In total confidence with the caller, I said of course and the date and time were set.

May 4, 2013, the session was. It proceeded beautifully and was very enlightening. As the message developed, there was a separate special invitation from Angel Raphael who invited me to connect on a regular basis weekly.

After the session, I invited Angel Raphael and the series of messages started. For the whole story, please visit http://angelraphaelspeaks.com/ and read about the Angel Raphael Speaks Series.

Some three hundred messages followed and were published as Angel Raphael Speaks Volumes 1, 2, 3 and then many books about healing. A special invitation came about message set 16 that invited me to visit prison energetically and bring feedback.

Eventually, that incentivized more writing totaling over 50 prison books including a new compilation that includes all earlier *Angel Raphael Speaks - Prisons* messages and eight messages about prison that came later. The title of that project is *Penitentiary Edition Angel Raphael* Speaks.

Before the invitation, the thrust of my life for the prior twenty years had been about teaching and practicing healing energy work, and my mission has been to reach the people. Angel Raphael is the Angel of Healing and the Invitation aligned very precisely with the work that I had been doing for years.

1 - Why I Am Writing This Book

I resisted the invitation to write about prisons and put it off. After starting, the flow has been quite dramatic. A vast list of titles I journaled also awaits my attention.

Events in the world seem to stimulate the thought bits that get delivered to my mind where they align in quite unique positions. I am frequently amazed by my thoughts, and others also ask if one thing or the other is inspired or channeled. It all seems to be quite fluid now.

When I lack a clear view of a title, I do some research so that clarity can surface. There is so much that seems obvious but is lost in the complexity and variation of ordinary things throughout the variety of locations where prisons are located.

My orientation of management is probably entirely different than most readers. I tend to take things quite literally, and that has been both an advantage and an impediment.

When I get answers, I usually ask more questions. "And?"

Also "Except?" Prisons are complicated in general, and that seems to be amplified by the requirement of a call for inclusiveness within me.

Unfortunately, entirely inclusive is a state of compliance which is easily requested but not as simple to achieve.

2 - The Power of Purpose

"Prison Rehabilitation

The answer to prison rehabilitation is purpose. While some institutions may have initiated programs to engage their residents, the feeling of a purposeful life brings a new reality to the incarcerated."

{First paragraph of Prison Rehabilitation from Message Set 10 of Angel Raphael Speaks. Full Message in Chapter 15 here}

3 - Prisons Seem to Amplify a Down Spiral for Prisoners

An Unintentional Slippery Slide

Fault

No

One

4 - Concept Books Show Options

Out of the Sixty books that I have written about prison, more than half have been concept books which have ideas that could be implemented over time in an efficient way.

In the process of writing these books, I became more and more aware of the complexity of writing about prison programs. There are a lot of prisons, and each facility has different prisoner needs.

Money is a challenge for changing the tasks at hand, and the absence of funds requires some repositioning of thought if the change is to happen.

One way to shift things could be the concept that I am now describing as segmentation. This is space use redefinition to add timed occupancy so that the population is spread around the building and around the clock.

Control of space and activities could bring an elongated sense of peace and spaciousness to those occupants who are willing to be cooperative with the suggestions and the actions that shift by the restructuring.

Segmentation can fulfill a flow control function when flexibility and teamwork are enabled.

5 - What Options Have No Cost

Complexity is pervasive as residents are there by the rule of law and there is little freedom to allow creativity that has not been previously approved. The rigidity is problematic for both efficiency and rehabilitation.

The only options that I see are rethinking of the rules in a progressive way to allow more opportunity for efficiency, rehabilitation, and kindness as the court orders are deliberately respected.

It could be more natural in modern times to be more sensitive and kind to prisoners while maintaining security. Society can legitimately change the rules by submitting appropriate proposals to the authorities who can seek the authorization from the voters.

The role of political representatives at all levels (Senators, Congressman, Governors, Mayors, Ward Leaders, etc.) are the proper authorities to hear your suggestions and bring proposals forward for legislative changes in the voting booth.

The high occupancy of prisons can aggravate problems and make answers seem non-existent. The closeness of prisoners can stress out everybody when space does not seem sufficient.

My earlier books have talked about space use that can help to dissipate tensions and optimize the amount of space per prisoner at every level of their day. Efficient space use can increase security and peace.

6 - Why Space Matters

You may have heard the expression "too many cooks spoil the soup." When too many people are trying to influence, control or work on a project, there can easily be a disagreement about the process.

When prisoners are crowded too close together, personal space may be little to non-existent, so it is easy to see how stress and confrontation can flare up.

I talk about space a lot and offer many ideas that could help, but there is a further complexity as there could be a significant cost to rethink and redo all the rules and processes in prisons throughout the land.

The option that makes sense to me is called Segmentation, and the essence of the idea is to control space differently than now so that prisons can have people up on three shifts and rotating in areas that would otherwise be empty at those times.

Spreading people out makes common sense. While there would likely not be funds available to create a lot of facility changes, the emphasis initially would be what can be done with existing resources administered differently.

Precise schedules and creative thinking.would be pivotal to success. The idea would be that creativity would be needed to justify any bits of structural change when possible.

The savings for physical facility changes must come in advance from the creativity that saves costs without facilities refitting.

7 - Why Time Matters

You may have heard the expressions:

"Time Waits for No Man (anon.)"

"Time Marches On (Anon.)"

Many wait for time to pass.

Waiting can be frustrating and aggravate residents and make trouble.

The Second is the basic unit of time.

The second unit of time is the minute which has 60 seconds.

The third unit of time is an hour which is 60 minutes or 3600 seconds.

The fourth unit of time is the day which has 24 hours or 86,400 seconds.

Reshuffling the fluidity of time and space for areas can reduce stress and maybe potential problems.

An Ounce of Prevention Is Worth a pound of Cure (anon.!)

Changing Time Patterns

When people flow without bottlenecks, clock watchers notice.

Can That Be Done Where You live?

Let's consider that you live in a pretty busy prison and that there are three significant blocks of time which vary by many things but let's assume that there are about sixteen hours of waking time and eight hours of cell time.

So let's invite prisoners to self-identify themselves as wanting to participate in a pattern that is different than the crowd. Some people who worked shifts on the outside may appreciate an opportunity for a B shift and C shift in prison.

Your prison can start from scratch and help to develop a unique pattern that works for your locale. Please start the conversation using approximately eight-hour time blocks for your possibility concept design explorations.

Try conceptualizing limited or no access to the cell blocks where other shifts are sleeping during newly selected shifts out of cell time so that the density minimization of the rest of the facility is maximized on a rotating flow basis throughout the full cycle of the variations.

The approximately eight-hour grouping is an arbitrary time block that suggests that we want to reset the space so that patterns can be proportional for up to one-third of the prisoners who may choose to if they find some benefit in shifts.

8 - Why Self-Determination Matters

The lack of individual freedom can be depressive to the human spirit. When lack happens, the status quo shifts. There can be an opportunity for a restructuring or paradigm shifting. The Resetting of patterns may be helpful or hurtful, it depends.

Anyone who has been in the military and went through boot camp knows that their awareness can shift in the process. Free citizens may not appreciate their freedom or any wasting of it that they do but restrict it, and they are ready to fight.

During the military indoctrination periods, there are trainers in your face challenging the perspective you have or living your life your way that contains a strong message of the way that they suggest would be better suited to your success while in the military.

Discipline is powerful when it becomes a natural factor in the pattern of thought that flows smoothly. Prison may be the right choice for society to help those who lack discipline and options.

Many moons ago there was a movie called the *Dirty Dozen* where prisoners were offered military opportunities that had them risking their lives, but it also provided them with the ability to make a choice. The dozen chose to make a decision.

Choosing a shift is a much less formidable option, but it is still a choice that gives a prisoner a chance at self-determination and the power to deselect a less than optimal position. Change can be harmful or useful, and the option to select could be welcomed, analyzed and evaluated.

9 - Shift Blocks

If your prison typically has something like sixteen hours of non-cell use alignment within the facility and eight hours of cell use alignment, then reconfiguration can provide redefined options for potentially interested prisoners.

The time blocks could take many different alignments internally as desired and agreeable with the administration and those wishing to participate.

The crucial piece of all of this is to move forward without an effort that needed funding. An interactive process would be optimal to the success of the idea.

A lack of cooperation would be honored, but the resident would still have a choice to keep the existing status quo, or not. Even transitional blocks of a couple of hours could begin to shift the freedom and flow within the facility.

Flow is essential in the quality of life. In your body, the flow of blood sustains life.

The flow of peaceful interaction with others sustains self-confidence. The stream of creative thought can keep one optimistic and cooperative.

Access to things natural and spiritual can bring a sense of order and peace.

10 - Thinking Change Can Create Hope

Absoluteness, or lack thereof, is a characteristic of prison thinking that could change everything. Those who declare in absolute terms that something will never work are prime candidates to be left out of startup efforts and the opportunities that might be contained therein.

Success will only happen if there can be:

- Possibility Thinking
- Creative Projections
- Long View Thinking
- Analytical Problem Solving
- Patience
- Persistence
- Sensitivity to Others' Suggestions
- Willingness to take the bull by the horns.
- Mastermind Teams
- Resourcefulness
- Team thinking
- Willingness to concede for the greater good.

11 - Skill Set Inventory

I have suggested in previous books that a skills roster be developed for those prisoners who are willing to share a list of their skills. The idea is revived here because developing opportunities without costs will require the skills of many people.

For transparency purposes, please be clear that it is unlikely that very many people will get an opportunity to participate in the immediate future. Signing up as soon as possible can be helpful to reward early endorsers by recognizing those who supported the concept earlier before all the benefits were clear.

It will cost signer-ups nothing but cooperation is an indicator that can show the administration a sincere willingness to improve their life options. It will also show a less than selfish desire to help others while there is no guarantee at all for the benefit of the signer.

Signing up also allows the skills to be on record for future efforts at developing more segments to benefit more people later.

12 - Single Unit Startup

"Inch by inch anything is a cinch (anon.)" An old saying that keeps the idea clear.

Making each effort as correctly as possible is very important as success will provide an incentive for making more attempts. With each project, a variety of individual concepts can be considered.

Should a project fail, there would be no need to cancel the concept as each effort can be individually applied to each request correctly or be allowed to fizzle out and be replaced.

The individual application is not limited as a benefit to that one person because the problem that needs remediation is the density collectively.

As one individual is decreased from the mass of humanity, the block of people is reduced as is the intensity of the density that stresses the facility's resources and endangers all who live and work there.

Personal attention to the needs of one person is entirely unusual in prisons, but it is a much easier way to approach mass diminution of the crowd that is already assembled. Individual care can:

- Reduces the numbers of people in a location
- Spread the possibility for increased opportunities.
- Increases the likelihood of Redicivism reductions
- Decrease stress

13 - Every Prison Can Work at Changing A Bit

Choose One or Many Goals for your Prison

Every Prison Can Work at Changing the Path for one Prisoner

Every Prison Can Work at Changing Recidivism

Every Prison Can Work at Changing Optimism

Every Prison Can Work at Changing Solitary

Every Prison Can Work at Changing Purpose

Every Prison Can Work at Changing Visitation

Every Prison Can Work at Changing Teamwork

Every Prison Can Work at Changing Cooperation

Every Prison Can Work at Changing Communication

Every Prison Can Work at Changing Prisoner Spousal Support

Every Prison Can Work at Changing Prisoner Children Support

Every Prison Can Work at Changing Staff Safety

Every Prison Can Work at Changing Staff Support

Every Prison Can Work at Changing Staff Teamwork

Every Prison Can Work at Changing Prisoner Relations

Every Prison Can Work at Changing Job Prospects

Every Prison Can Work at Changing Education Opportunities

Every Prison Can Work at Changing Visitation Simplicity

Every Prison Can Work at Changing_____

& More

14 - Visitation & Motivation

There seems to be a big struggle to communicate and relate to the world outside the walls. Aware of that, prison staff can embrace and repurpose the motivation for growth and rehabilitation.

Of course, the word **can** is conditional on behalf of many participants who are both staff and residents. Like many things in life, there is a way to organize events so that cooperation is most likely.

Both groups have some capacity for flexibility when circumstances are aligned in a way that they are inclined to favor. A huge component of the inclination can be rooted in the way that topics are presented.

If each participant can focus a bit and list the results they want, there can be a goal list developed. Both groups could then construct a list of their view of what those on the other side of the issue are most likely to think.

When you have both lists, you can sit down with your colleagues and endeavor to present ideas in the best alignment with the desires of the other team. Then you can reset your priorities to establish an opening position, a negotiating perspective and the limits of your flexibility.

Success or failure may be determined by the way that your team can be flexible and also sensitive to the deal-breakers from the opposing teams perspective. Skillful negotiators can avoid collapse and claim success.

15 - Prison Rehabilitation
. {From Angel Raphael Speaks Message Set 10}

Prison Rehabilitation

The answer to prison rehabilitation is purpose. While some institutions may have initiated programs to engage their residents, the feeling of a purposeful life brings a new reality to the incarcerated.

Purposes to consider will be ones that work for the incarcerated as well as the society which actually pays the bills. Special characteristics to include would be the creation of a feeling of accomplishment generated by prisoner effort and drastic cost savings for the institution.

The real loss to prisons is wasted time, no productivity and no graciousness of interactive genius. If invited, the right use of time can provide different results than now seen.

There is no profit to society when cruelness is applied to the control of citizens. There may be temporary security, but that comes at a big price to the potential of all.

The best way to learn about what is possible is to listen to the troubled stories of the incarcerated people. Their genius can be tapped by mining information about how to fill the gap that they slipped in to so that newer walkers on their path can find the hole filled by their charity of sharing their pain as a love patch to the sinkholes of society.

The answers through this channel are coming differently than most could conceive and that is because neither you nor I have a job whose agenda has its own needs.

You ask to imagine how much can be cut from prison costs to maintain security, improve lives, create new industry and improve the focus, flavor, and flair of American life and you dowsed for an answer. You got 47% reduction, and you questioned your dowsing. Your questioning is wise because there is a vast industry that has roots in the status quo.

While that is true, your answer has potential that will serve the ones that would resist the initiatives that flow from the message. Their positions are survivable as is for a time unknown but their openness to change can also serve their security.

The change will happen even if they choose to use their money to resist the inevitable avalanche of change. Their opportunities are paramount in the areas of personal safety for all and the possibility to create new meaningful arrangements that are self-sustaining for all levels of the resident base and those employed in the industry.   ARS 10

16 - Prisoner Prayer

{From Chapter 3 in Prison Prayer Book}

Prayer Can Change the One Praying

{Prayer Between the one Praying and the Creator is optimal without observers or agendas}

Persons who set out to pray can be engaged at various levels. Some people may pray as they were taught as a child and that may or may not be advantageous.

You are not a child, and God respects that so much that each is given FREE WILL. We get to make our own decisions.

Are You in EGO or AGO?
EGO = Easing God Out
AGO = A Growth Opportunity

What you are thinking at every moment has a lot to do with where you are in your life and where you can go. Who and what you focus on impacts upon all that you are able to accomplish.

If you are focused on getting or receiving from God or others, then your relationship with God may be out of balance, and that is entirely up to you. Everybody has God on your side.

Every child of God has that excellent support, and it has fantastic potential. What you do or have done has an impact on all that was or still is to be manifested.

Who you were is not an absolute final determination of who you are and who you can be. Who would you pray to be?

Who will you be? We get to make up our own minds. Consider Prison Prayer Book or http:www.Create-A-Prayer.com for help.

17 - Prayer Suggestion For Staff

{From the Book *Emergency Medical Kindness In The Cradle of Liberty: Big City – Cracked Bell*}

Prayer Suggestions for Police, Fire, Ambulance, Paramedics, Medical Practitioners and Emergency Service Workers, and Correction Officers

God Almighty

I/We recognize you as the source of all good, all healing, all wholeness, all wellness and all support for your offspring in all matters.

I/We unify with your Divine Will and strive to serve your children in all their needs with the same dignity and respect that you do. We appreciate your direction, guidance, and protection as we go out to love and nurture all your people in their time of need.

I/We claim our highest skilled functioning under your guidance and our ability to hear the things to do, the words to say and the seeds to plant. I/We claim the healings we will see today are now optimized as this claim is declared and we claim all this or better now.

I/We accept that the optimized care of those in need is started, increased and fulfilled now.

I/we offer my/our sincere Thanks to you Dear God, AND SO IT IS.

18 - Envision Please an Up Spiral to Help Prisoners Be Stars

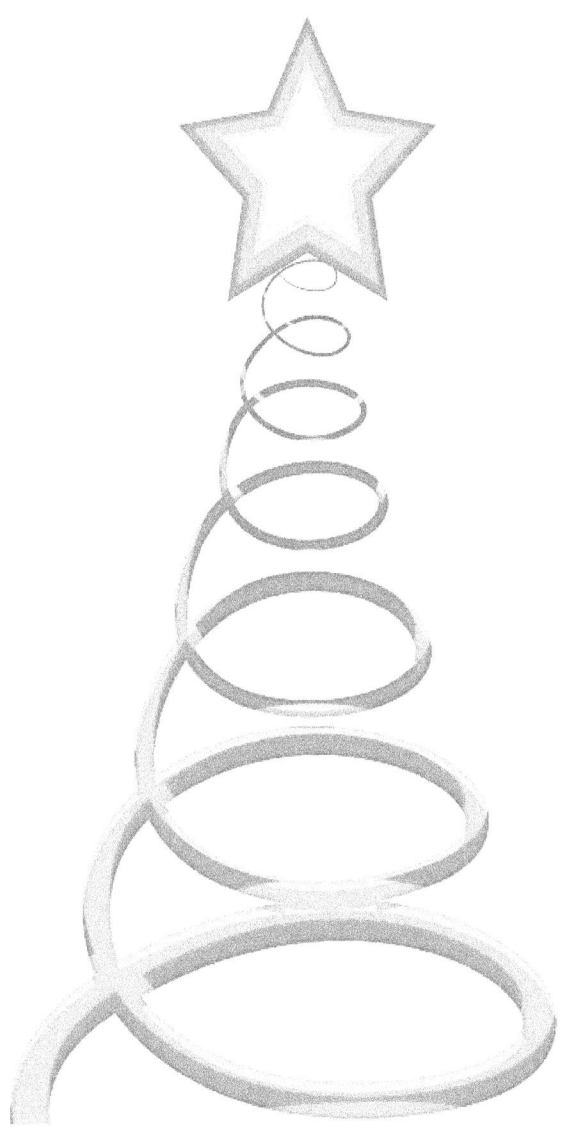

19 - Wrap Up

I remain hopeful that the day will come when Prisoners, Prison Staff, Administration, Politicians, Legislators, Governors, Taxpayers and the President can see the potential in purpose, prayer and positive perceptions of prison possibilities.

The late Dr. Wayne W. Dyer could see the power of belief and wrote a book about it in 2001. The Title is *You'll See It When You Believe It: The Way to Your Personal Transformation.*

May all who read this be blessed AND SO IT IS!

Rev. Mike Wanner

20 - Thank You

For

Considering

These

Ideas

21 - Don't Worry Ever

Ever

It Does Not Help Prayer Still Does!

Resource: http://Create-A-Prayer.com

22 - Books Category Resources at www.Amazon.com

Distant Healing (or Mail List) e-mail mikewann@voicenet.com

Veterans Healing Six Pack plus 2
http://angelraphaelspeaks.com/healing-books/veterans/

PTSD Power Pack
http://angelraphaelspeaks.com/healing-books/ptsd/

Angel Raphael Speaks Series & Other Angel Books
http://angelraphaelspeaks.com/

Reiki
http://angelraphaelspeaks.com/healing-books/reiki/

Children
http://angelraphaelspeaks.com/healing-books/children/

Emergency Medical Kindness
http://angelraphaelspeaks.com/healing-books/emergency-medical-kindness/

Cancer
http://angelraphaelspeaks.com/healing-books/cancer/

Addictions
http://angelraphaelspeaks.com/healing-books/addictions/

Miscellaneous Healing
http://angelraphaelspeaks.com/healing-books/misc-healing/

Prison Books - 50+ Prison Books
http://angelraphaelspeaks.com/prison-books/

23 - Angels Please Prayers

Addict's

Angels of Healing Selected
Help Me to Stay Directed
Come To Me From The Sky
I Am Ready to Succeed Not Try
If I Don't Invite You In
I Might Not Win
I Have Been Lost For Too Long
Help Me To Stay Strong

Alcoholic's

Angels of Healing On High
Help Me to Stay Dry
Come To Me From The Sky
I Am Ready to Succeed Not Try
If I Don't Invite You In
I Might Not Win
I Have Been Lost For Too Long
Help Me To Stay Strong

From

http://AngelRaphaelSpeaks.com/AAAAAAA/
The Link Above Has the Core Messages from the book on drop-down pages.

24 - Private Channeling

Angel Raphael Speaks a series of free messages that are channeled through Reverend Mike Wanner for the Highest good and Highest Healing of all concerned.

Many questions arise about Reverend Mike doing private channeling, and he does help with that so E-mail him.

Reverend Mike is available worldwide as a psychic channel, emotional release facilitator, spiritual energy practitioner & teacher, and public speaker. He looks forward to meeting you soon! Email - mikewann@voicenet.com 215-342-1270

PRIVATE SPIRITUAL READINGS/channelings or Spiritual Healing Sessions: Telephone or in person.

Rev. Mike is available for individual, intuitive one-on-one sessions with you, his Guide Family, and your Guides. He helps by offering clarity on emotional situations about your life, your purpose, your spirituality, and your release of stuffed emotions and cellular memory.

Connect to the love of your Guides today!

For more information, Please visit

http://angelraphaelspeaks.com/channel/

25 - Reverend Mike Wanner

Rev. Mike Wanner started his spiritual and ministerial studies with Reiki in 1993 and had studied seven styles of Reiki in the U.S., Japan, Canada, Denmark and Australia. He is certified to teach. He became certified to teach Integrated Energy Therapy in 1999 and co-taught the first IET class of the new Millennium. Mike began dowsing in 2001.

Ordained as an Interfaith Minister of the Circle of Miracles Ministry and a Metaphysical Minister of the International Metaphysical Ministry, Rev. Mike practices and teaches spiritual energy therapies in the Philadelphia Area.

Rev. Mike holds ministerial degrees from the University of Metaphysics and the University of Sedona. He is a Pastoral Care Associate at Jefferson - Frankford Hospital. He taught at the National Academy of Massage Therapy and Health Sciences.

Rev. Mike was a faculty member of the Medical Mission Sister's Center for Human Integration's School of Integrated Body/Mind Therapies in Fox Chase, Philadelphia, PA for twelve years.

For a complete Biography, Please visit
http://ReverendMikeWanner.com/Bio